WHY DOES THE MOON CHANGE SHAPE?

BY ISAAC ASIMOV

Gareth Stevens Children's Books
MILWAUKEE

For a free color catalog describing Gareth Stevens' list of high-quality children's books, call 1-800-341-3569 (USA) or 1-800-461-9120 (Canada).

Library of Congress Cataloging-in-Publication Data

Asimov, Isaac, 1920-
    Why does the moon change shape? / by Isaac Asimov. — A Gareth Stevens Children's
Books ed.
       p. cm. — (Ask Isaac Asimov)
    Includes bibliographical references and index.
    Summary: Explains why the moon changes from crescent to full moon every twenty-nine
and one-half days.
    ISBN 0-8368-0438-4
    1. Moon—Phases—Juvenile literature. [1. Moon—Phases.] I. Title. II. Series: Asimov,
Isaac, 1920- Ask Isaac Asimov.
    QB588.A85 1991
    523.3'2—dc20   90-25430

A Gareth Stevens Children's Books edition

Edited, designed, and produced by
Gareth Stevens Children's Books
1555 North RiverCenter Drive, Suite 201
Milwaukee, Wisconsin 53212, USA

Picture Credits
pp. 2-3, National Optical Astronomy Observatories; pp. 4-5, Frank Zullo, © 1989; pp. 6-7, Julian Baum; pp. 8-9, Regis
Lefebure/Third Coast, © 1990; p. 9 (inset), Keith Ward; pp. 10-11, Hale Observatories; pp. 10-11 (background),
National Optical Astronomy Observatories; pp. 12-13, Keith Ward; p. 14, © Gareth Stevens, Inc.; p. 15, © Tom
Miller; p. 16 (inset), © Gareth Stevens, Inc.; pp. 16-17, © William P. Sterne, Jr.; p. 18, Frank Zullo, © 1985; p. 19,
courtesy of NASA; p. 21, Bishop Museum; pp. 22-24, Rick Karpinski/DeWalt and Associates

Cover, Frank Zullo, © 1985: A full Moon hovering near the horizon on a dark Arizona night.

Series editor: Elizabeth Kaplan
Series designer: Sabine Huschke
Picture researcher: Daniel Helminak
Assistant picture researcher: Diane Laska
Consulting editor: Matthew Groshek

Printed in MEXICO

1 2 3 4 5 6 7 8 9 97 96 95 94 93 92 91

Contents

Words that appear in the glossary are printed in **boldface** type the first time they occur in the text.

A World of Questions

Our world is full of strange and beautiful things. The night sky glimmers with stars. Lightning branches from huge clouds during a thunderstorm. Sometimes we have questions about things around us. Asking questions helps us appreciate the many wonders of the Universe.

For instance, have you noticed that the **Moon** changes shape from one night to the next? Sometimes it's a beautiful circle of light. Sometimes it's only half a circle. Sometimes it's just a sliver. Why does this happen? Let's find out.

Dancing in the Moonlight

The Moon is a round, rocky world. It has tall mountains. It has deep **craters**. We see these features because the Sun shines its light on the Moon.

The Moon does not produce its own light. It appears to shine because of the sunlight bouncing off its surface. This light is **reflected** back to Earth as moonlight. The Moon's silvery light sparkling on a field of snow makes winter nights seem lonely and mysterious. The glow of the **harvest Moon** makes autumn nights seem soft and warm.

6

Sun

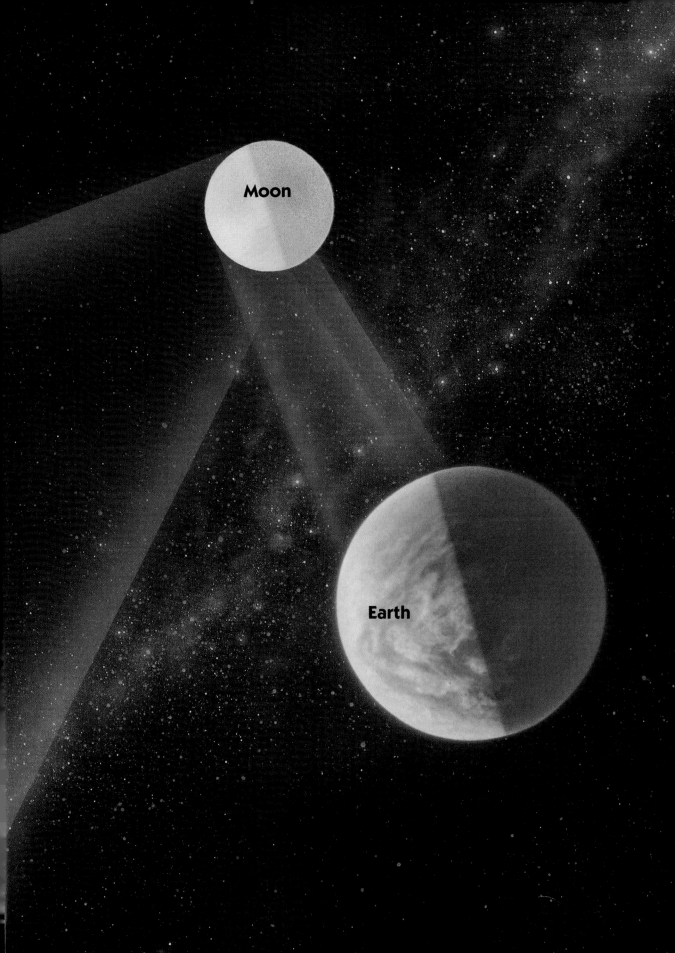

The Moon's Changing Faces

Although the Moon is a **sphere**, it doesn't always look like one. In fact, it seems to change shape every night. Sometimes you might see the Moon as a round orange ball rising in the sky. Sometimes you might see it as a silver wedge among the stars. You might notice it as a pockmarked half circle, hanging in the sky during the day. Or you might not be able to find the Moon at all. We call these different shapes of the Moon its **phases**.

The Names of the Moon

The phases of the Moon have different names. When the Moon looks like a round ball, it is called a full Moon. When it is just a sliver, we call it a crescent Moon.

10

full Moon

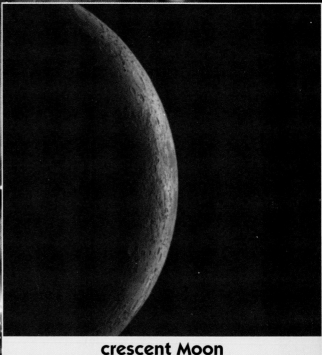

crescent Moon

When the Moon appears as a half-circle wedge, we call it a half Moon. When the Moon is between half and full, it is called a gibbous Moon. When we can't see the Moon at all, we call it a new Moon.

half Moon

gibbous Moon

Phase In, Phase Out

The Moon goes through all of its phases in about 29 days. Beginning as a new Moon, it grows to a crescent Moon, a half Moon, a gibbous Moon, and then a full Moon. This process takes just over two weeks. During this time, we say that the Moon is **waxing**.

Over the next two weeks, the full Moon shrinks. It becomes a gibbous Moon, a half Moon, a crescent, and finally disappears, becoming a new Moon again. During this time, we say that the Moon is **waning**. The picture shows some of the Moon's phases as it waxes and wanes.

From Sunlight to Shadow

If you shine a light on a round object, such as a ball, half of the ball will be in light and half will be in shadow. The same thing happens when the Sun shines on the Moon.

As seen from space, the Moon is always half in sunlight and half in shadow. The outer ring of the diagram below shows this. The inner ring shows how the Moon looks from Earth. During a full Moon, we see the entire face of the Moon lit by the Sun. During a new Moon, the side of the Moon facing us is entirely in shadow. Between these times, we see different amounts of the Moon's face lit up. This is why the Moon changes shape.

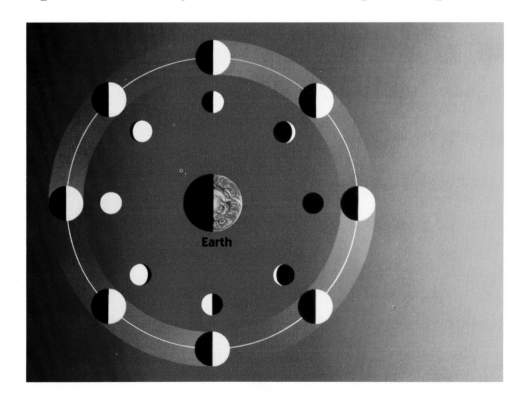

Earth

Now You See It, Now You Don't

Many calendars show dates when the Moon will be in different phases. But, on any given night, you may have to check the sky at different times to find the Moon. Sometimes the Moon rises early in the evening. At other times, it rises later at night.

This picture shows the crescent Moon and the planet **Venus** setting over a city. The photographer took the picture over several hours. During that time, the Moon and Venus sank lower and lower in the sky.

			1	2	3	4	5
6 Half Moon	7	8	9	10	11	12	
13	14	New Moon 15	16	17	18	19	
20	21	22	Half Moon 23	24	25	26	
27	28	29	Full Moon 30	31			

Going through a Phase

The Moon isn't the only **heavenly body** that seems to change shape when viewed from Earth. **Mercury**, shown right, and Venus also go through phases. These planets sometimes pass between Earth and the Sun. For this reason, we see different amounts of their surfaces lit up when they are in different places in their orbits.

Sometimes Mercury and Venus look like full circles of light. Other times, they appear as crescents. But you can only see the phases if you view these planets through a telescope.

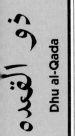

Dhu al-Hijjah

Of Time, the Moon, and the Seasons

People sometimes use calendars based on the phases of the Moon. Such calendars are called lunar calendars. In a lunar calendar, the new Moon marks the beginning of each month. Most years have twelve months, but some years have thirteen months. Adding an extra month keeps lunar calendars in step with the seasons. The Hebrew calendar and the Islamic calendar are lunar calendars. The names of the months in the Islamic calendar are shown around the edges of these pages.

Islamic astronomers, such as those shown to the right, kept close watch on the Moon and other heavenly bodies to make sure that their calendars remained accurate.

The calendar people commonly use today is based on the seasons, not on the phases of the Moon. But the divisions of the calendar are still called months, after the Moon.

Dhu al-Qada

Ruler of the Night Sky

The Moon has always been an object of beauty and wonder. Today we know more about the Moon than ever before. Many spacecraft have flown by it, and astronauts have hopped around on its surface. But the Moon still holds charm and mystery for us whenever we gaze at its changing faces.

More Books to Read

The Earth's Moon by Isaac Asimov (Gareth Stevens)
The Moon Seems to Change by Barbara Emberley and Ed Emberley
     (Harper & Row Junior Books)
The Space Spotter's Guide by Isaac Asimov (Gareth Stevens)

Places to Write

Here are some places you can write to for more information about
the Moon. Be sure to tell them exactly what you want to know.
Give them your full name and address so that they can write back
to you.

About the Moon:

National Space Society
600 Maryland Avenue SW
Washington, D.C. 20024

Space Communications Branch
Ministry of State for Science
     and Technology
240 Sparks Street
C. D. Howe Building
Ottawa, Ontario   K1A 1A1

About missions to the Moon:

NASA Kennedy Space Center
Educational Services Office
Kennedy Space Center,
     Florida   32899

Glossary

crater (KRATE-er): a hole on a planet or moon that forms when a
     meteorite strikes it or when a volcano explodes.

harvest Moon: the full Moon that occurs nearest to September 21.

heavenly body: any star, planet, natural satellite, or other natural object that is found in space.

Mercury (MUR-kyur-ee): the planet closest to the Sun.

Moon: the heavenly body that circles Earth.

phase (faze): a change that usually occurs as part of a cycle, such as the changing faces of the Moon.

reflect (ree-FLEHKT): to bounce back; light reflects off the Moon's surface and travels to Earth.

sphere (sfear): an object that is round like a ball.

Venus (VEE-nuhs): the second planet from the Sun; Venus is the planet closest to Earth.

wane: to grow smaller or shrink; the Moon wanes when it goes from a full Moon to a new Moon.

wax (wacks): to grow larger; the Moon waxes when it goes from a new Moon to a full Moon.

Index